"The purpose of life is to contribute in some way to making things better."

— Robert F. Kennedy

For Paula and Rubin and Robin and Kara,
and Steven and Janie,
and Ken and David and Tatyana,
and for all those whose hands
and hearts reach out in the service
of justice, and story. — D.W.

Text copyright © 2022 by Deborah Wiles
Illustrations copyright © 2022 by Tatyana Fazlalizadeh

Library of Congress Cataloging-in-Publication Data available
ISBN 978-0-545-17123-6
10 9 8 7 6 5 4 3 2 1   22 23 24 25 26
Printed in China 62
First edition, September 2022

Book design by Charles Kreloff

The text type was set in Clarendon.
The illustrations were rendered in graphite and digital color.

BOBBY

A STORY OF ROBERT F. KENNEDY

By Deborah Wiles

Illustrations by Tatyana Fazlalizadeh

SCHOLASTIC PRESS / NEW YORK

Grandfather said:

Back in the days when people worked with their hands, in the days before spaceships and televisions and computers, Robert Francis Kennedy was born.

All his life, he loved ice cream and big dogs. Just like you do.

There were rich people and poor people in America then, just like today, and a lot of people in between.

Robert's family was wealthy, so Robert grew up a rich boy, the seventh of nine children, small and awkward and shy. His father, Joe, pushed his children to be tough and fierce, to reach out their hands and grab at victory, to WIN at everything. Everything. That's just who Joe was. "We don't want any losers around here!" he shouted.

Robert wanted to please his father and to be fierce and strong and ferocious. So one day, when his family was on their boat not too far from shore, he jumped overboard to prove he could outswim his brothers. Soon, he began to flail and splash and sink.

"He can't swim!" yelled his brother Jack.
"I'll get him!" yelled his brother Joe Jr.

Even though he came in last in family competitions, even though he was prone to accidents because he was trying so hard, Robert tried harder than anyone else in his family to win. Once, when rushing to dinner and trying to outrun his sisters, he ran straight into a glass door! The glass shattered all around him, and Robert ended up with stitches.

Still, he pretended to be tough and fierce on the outside. Just like
you . . . sometimes. But on the inside, where his heart beat steadily
and his feelings simmered and bubbled, Robert was thoughtful
and gentle and, often, afraid. Just like you, maybe?

Sometimes, when Joe Kennedy was disappointed in his young
son's shyness and awkwardness, he bellowed, "Runt!" But
Robert's mother, Rose, knew better. She knew that Robert's
strength lay in his heart.

But Robert didn't know that yet. So, in school, he used his fists to fight anyone who called him names. Even in college, when he was too small to play football, he played anyway. He grabbed that football with both hands and kept on playing, tough as nails, even when he broke his leg in the tackle! Oh, how he wanted to WIN.

Soon came the days of astronauts and rock and roll and marching for justice, equality, and civil rights for all Americans. Robert's big brother Jack — John Fitzgerald Kennedy — wanted to become president of the United States. He asked Robert to manage his campaign.

Robert, who loved his brother Jack with a mighty heart, worked tougher and harder than anyone and scored a victory for his brother in the 1960 presidential election. It felt so good to WIN!

Robert saw the world the way his father had taught him to see it: There were winners and there were losers. There was no in-between. But as you know, the world is full of in-between.

Robert was appointed head of the Justice Department as attorney general of the United States. He became President Kennedy's closest confidante and advisor. Their work for social justice and civil rights was cautious at first (too cautious, their critics said), but the events of the Civil Rights Movement demanded change, and so did the American people.

Robert committed the Justice Department to that change. "On this generation of Americans falls the full burden of proving to the world that we really mean it when we say that all men are created free and equal before the law."

He wrote to Jack, his brother, "The most significant civil rights problem is voting." As he worked with Americans who were risking their lives in the thick of the Civil Rights Movement, he began to understand that winning was more than steamrolling over everyone else for your own victory.

A peaceful home in a safe neighborhood, a satisfying job, a good education, and equal protection and justice under the law—this was winning, and every American deserved to win. "We know that law is the glue that holds civilization together," he said. "And we know that if one man's rights are denied, the rights of all others are endangered."

Then, suddenly, on November 22, 1963, someone in Dallas, Texas, shot and killed Jack, Robert's brother, the president. America was lost and Robert could not be consoled. He kept his job as attorney general with a new president, Lyndon Johnson, and then resigned after the passage of the Civil Rights Act of 1964, legislation he had urged his brother to support. Then Robert Kennedy disappeared into his sadness.

But the voices of the American people grew louder.

JIM CROW MUST GO!

Maybe there was work to do here, in concert with others who were already on the front lines of America, changing things for the better. Maybe he could be useful. Maybe.

And so, after a time of deep, dark mourning, sheltered from the world save for his faith and his family, Robert Kennedy — still thoughtful and gentle inside, still afraid sometimes — made a decision to reenter the world. And in that decision, he became truly tough and fierce, because he became strong of heart. Just as his mother, Rose, knew he would.

These days, as you know, the United States is fighting a war in Vietnam, where Americans and Vietnamese families and soldiers are dying. And dying. And dying. Robert wanted to end the war.

". . . a total military victory is not within sight or around the corner . . . in fact, it is probably beyond our grasp; and . . . the effort to win such a victory will only result in the further slaughter of thousands of innocent and helpless people — a slaughter which will forever rest on our national conscience . . . the best way to save our most precious stake in Vietnam — the lives of our soldiers — is to stop the enlargement of the war, and . . . the best way to end casualties is to end the war."

— Robert F. Kennedy, February 1968

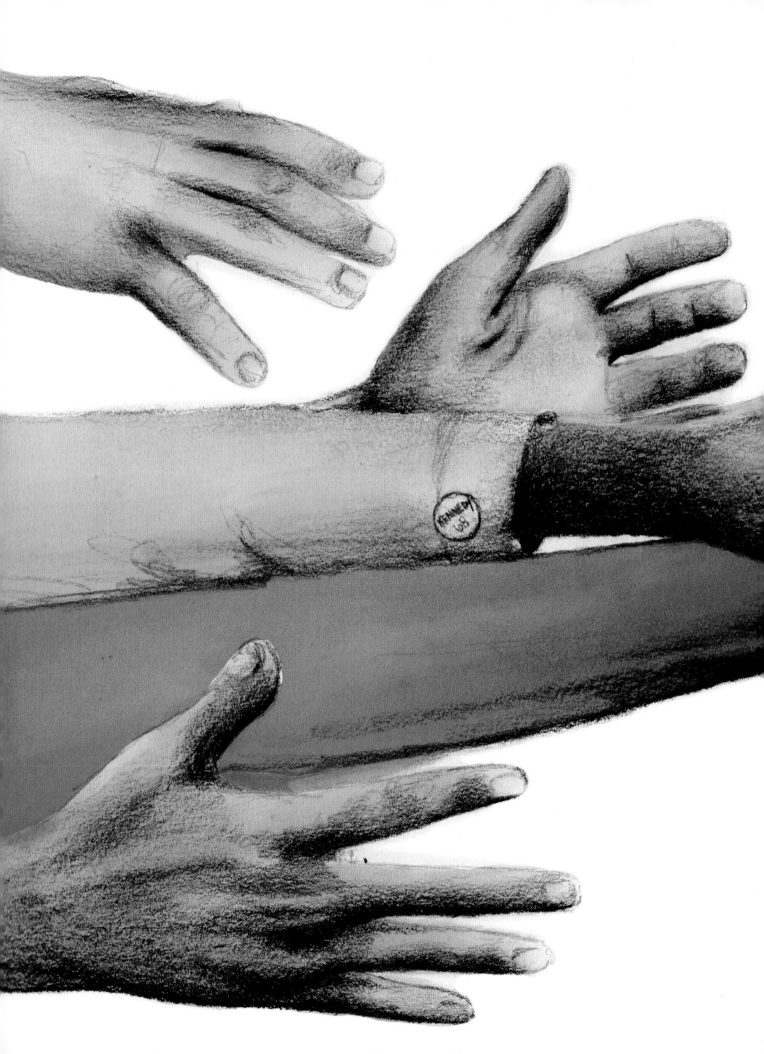

So, after serving as a United States senator from
New York, Robert decided to run for president of
the United States himself, just as his brother Jack
had done. This time, he didn't grab at victory to
win. Instead, he reached out his hand.

And do you know what happened? Hands of all colors,
hands in all neighborhoods, hands of all sizes . . .
Hands reached back to him. Americans claimed Robert
Francis Kennedy as one of their own.

They called him Bobby.

While he campaigned to become president, Bobby traveled to meet the American people, the people whose stories had changed him, just as his losses had changed him. He understood now that his job, in this time and place, was to serve the people, to champion their good work, to ask questions, and to help change what he could.

He often ended his conversations with, "We can do better than this."

He spoke to college students at universities across the country about the Vietnam War and poverty and hunger and a world yearning for justice; he challenged them to get involved in civic life and change. He ate supper with coal-mining families of Appalachia; he rode down a country road in Indiana, and a telephone lineman on a pole across the field swung his yellow hard hat hello; children streamed from a nearby elementary school to greet him.

"I do not run for the presidency merely to oppose any man but to propose new policies. I run because I am convinced that this country is on a perilous course and because I have such strong feelings about what must be done, and I feel that I'm obliged to do all that I can."

— Robert F. Kennedy, March 1968

He always wore his shyness next to his heart, so while campaigning in Los Angeles, California, he knelt next to a shy child in the Watts neighborhood and said, "My little girl wears glasses, too, and I love her very much."

He met with migrant fruit pickers in New York and farmworkers in California and listened to their stories of overcrowded homes, minuscule pay, and dangerous working conditions. He was so angered by what he saw that he embraced their cause and their commitment to nonviolent protest as they worked to form a farmworkers union. "What do you need?" he asked them. "And how can I help?"

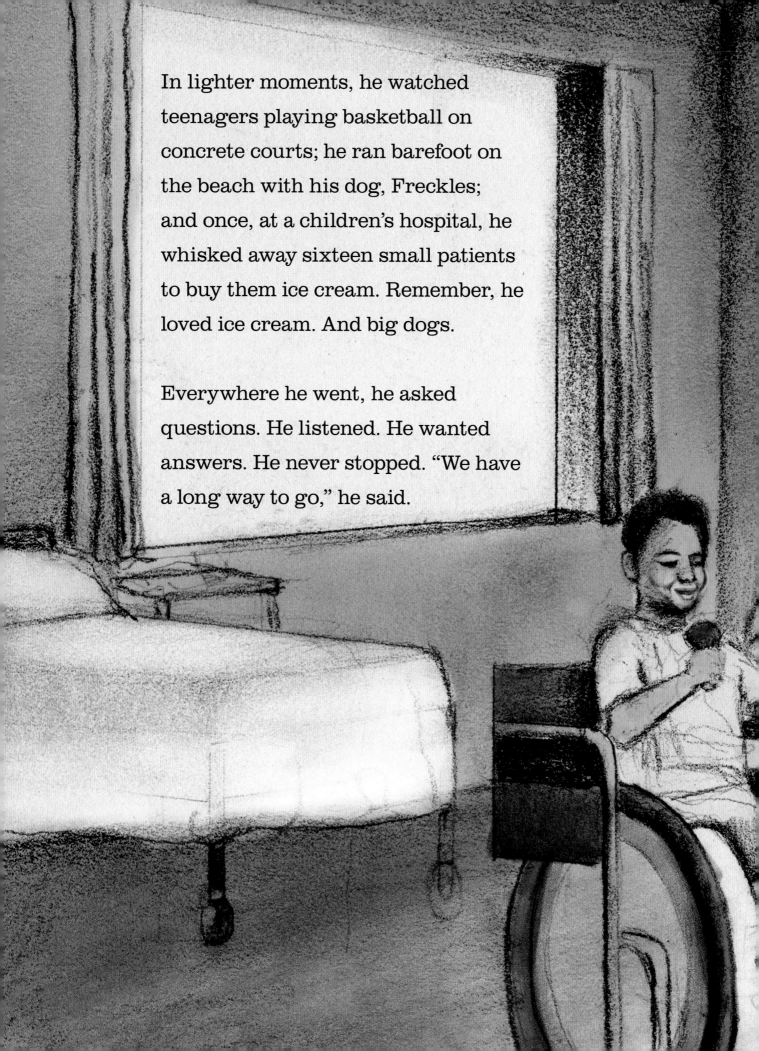

In lighter moments, he watched teenagers playing basketball on concrete courts; he ran barefoot on the beach with his dog, Freckles; and once, at a children's hospital, he whisked away sixteen small patients to buy them ice cream. Remember, he loved ice cream. And big dogs.

Everywhere he went, he asked questions. He listened. He wanted answers. He never stopped. "We have a long way to go," he said.

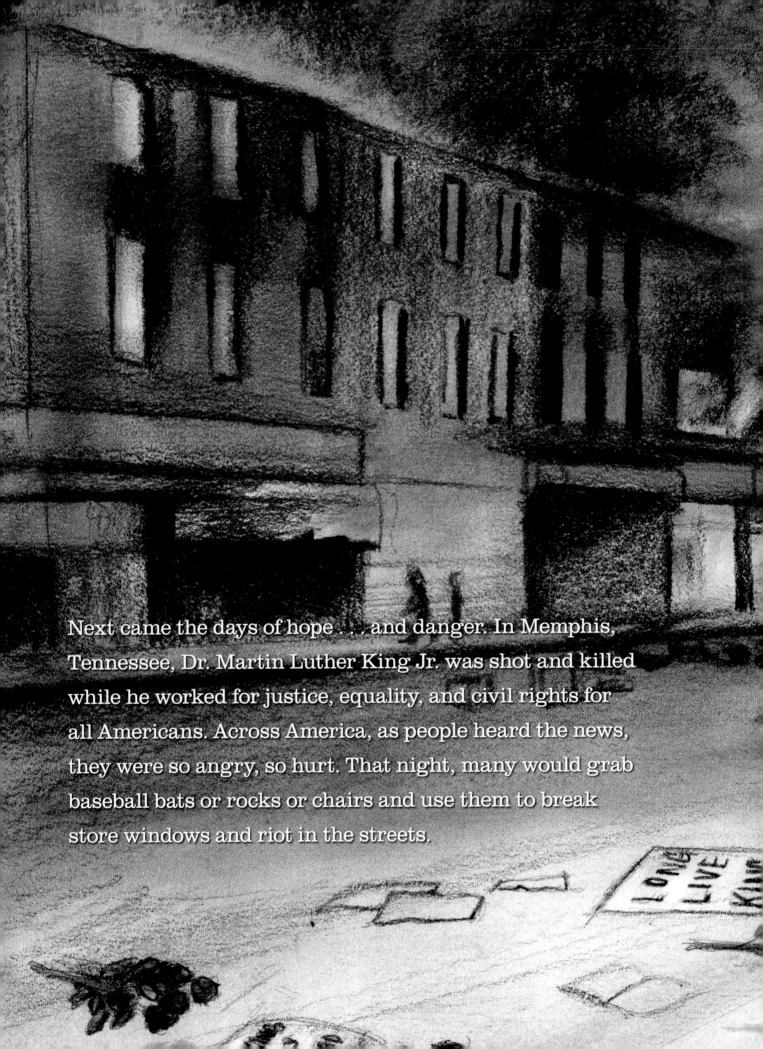

Next came the days of hope . . . and danger. In Memphis,
Tennessee, Dr. Martin Luther King Jr. was shot and killed
while he worked for justice, equality, and civil rights for
all Americans. Across America, as people heard the news,
they were so angry, so hurt. That night, many would grab
baseball bats or rocks or chairs and use them to break
store windows and riot in the streets.

Bobby was on a plane that afternoon, on the way to Indianapolis, Indiana, to campaign for president, when he heard the news. When he landed, instead of talking to the people about becoming president, he stood on the back of a flatbed truck as darkness fell, and broke the news about Dr. King's death.

WHERE DO WE GO FROM HERE?

He was nervous but determined. His hands shook,
the way they often did when he spoke, so he held on
to the notes that were written for him by a friend on
the plane, but he did not use them. Instead, he spoke
from his heart. He started like this:

"I have bad news for you, for all of our fellow citizens, and people who love peace all over the world." The people were shocked, stunned, full of anger and grief. Bobby told them, "I feel in my own heart the same kind of feeling. I had a member of my family killed . . ." Yes, people remembered that. Of course.

Then Bobby asked the people in Indiana to rise above their grief and anger.

> "What we need in the United States is not division; what we need in the United States is not hatred; what we need in the United States is not violence and lawlessness, but is love, and wisdom, and compassion toward one another, and a feeling of justice toward those who still suffer within our country, whether they be White or whether they be Black."

Cities across the United States were on fire that night, but Indianapolis was not one of them. Some said it was Bobby who made that happen, but it was the people of Indianapolis, who lived together and worked together, like we do, and made the decision to be peaceful together and work for change. And Bobby, that night, offered them his heart.

Robert Francis Kennedy did not become president of the United States. Sixty-three days after Dr. King was killed, Bobby was shot and killed in Los Angeles, California, by an angry man with a gun.

How do you live with a thing like that? First, you come to say thank you, and good-bye.

Look at all of us here, lining this long stretch of railroad tracks, all of us different, some young, some old, some carrying babies or baseball gloves or flags or signs, all of us carrying so much sadness . . . and so much love.

So stand up straight. Put your hand over your heart. Here comes the train carrying Bobby Kennedy to Washington, DC, to be buried at Arlington National Cemetery.

Good-bye, Bobby. Good-bye.

Grandfather said:

Look around you. We have come here together in peace, in respect, and with common purpose. We know we have work to do.

These can be the days of hope and togetherness!

It will take many hands reaching out . . . just like yours.

It will take tough, fierce, mighty hearts . . . just like yours.

So ask questions.

Listen.

Learn.

Grow.

Get ready to change the world.

A Note About This Book:

You will find (if you haven't already) that it is hard to write about your heroes without making them out to be all good, or all-knowing, or all-everything to everyone. It's more truthful and meaningful to track their life stories, their stumbles and tragedies and triumphs, to see how they came to believe the values they held in the time they lived, and how those values led to choices that contributed to good in the world.

Robert Francis Kennedy was born on November 20, 1925, and died by an assassin's bullet on June 6, 1968. In his 42 years, he grew from a child of great privilege, who could have chosen a life of ease, into a man who made tough, principled choices through a life of service, a life that changed him and that inspired others to action and change.

He was not perfect. None of us is. His gift, to my mind, was his ability to rise up after losses and mistakes, to speak aloud hard truths, to champion the determination of others, and to help ease some of the pain and suffering and injustice he saw as he worked with others in communities, in Congress, and across this country in many different roles, including as United States attorney general during his brother's administration, as a United States senator from New York, as a husband and father, and as a presidential candidate. "What we need in the United States . . ."

I was fifteen years old the night Robert Kennedy was shot at the Ambassador Hotel in Los Angeles, California, just minutes after delivering a victory speech in the California Democratic presidential primary of 1968. I sat up for hours, hoping to hear he had made it through the night. The entire country mourned his passing, and I was among the inconsolable.

On June 8, 1968, over a million people, young and old, of all classes and races and identities and abilities, crowded together on railroad station platforms in cities and scattered themselves across fields through the rural countryside. They lined the 225-mile stretch of railroad tracks between New York City and Washington, DC, to pay homage to Robert Kennedy as a train carried him from his funeral mass at St. Patrick's Cathedral in Manhattan to Arlington National Cemetery in Virginia, where he was laid to rest near his brother Jack.

You can read more about the funeral train and see photos and footage of the people lining the tracks at https://time.com/longform/rfk-funeral-train-photos and by searching the "RFK funeral train" on YouTube.

In this story, I hope you get a sense of the man and the many people whose lives he touched — including mine — and continues to inspire through his legacy.

"The future is not a gift. It is an achievement. Every generation helps make its own future. This is the essential challenge of the present."
— Robert F. Kennedy

Further Reading

To learn more about Bobby's life and work, a good place to begin is at the John F. Kennedy Presidential Library, here: https://www.jfklibrary.org/learn/about-jfk/the-kennedy-family/robert-f-kennedy.

You can read Bobby's impromptu speech in Indianapolis, Indiana, upon the death of the Reverend Dr. Martin Luther King Jr. here: https://www.jfklibrary.org/learn/about-jfk/the-kennedy-family/robert-f-kennedy/robert-f-kennedy-speeches/statement-on-assassination-of-martin-luther-king-jr-indianapolis-indiana-april-4-1968. The remarks were filmed that fateful night, and you can watch here, on YouTube, at the Robert F. Kennedy Human Rights channel: https://www.youtube.com/watch?v=A2kWIa8wSC0.

Some of the incidents related in this book are taken from eulogies given at RFK's funeral mass and in print, gathered in a book called "An Honorable Profession": A Tribute to Robert F. Kennedy. I recommend it highly, to get a sense of Robert Kennedy's life and legacy, to be inspired, and to understand that every grown-up hero was a child just like you, full of feelings and fears, favorites and fun, brimming with questions, and determined to find the answers.

Partial Bibliography

Algeo, Matthew. *All This Marvelous Potential: Robert Kennedy's 1968 Tour of Appalachia*. Chicago: Chicago Review Press, 2020.

American Experience: RFK (2004). David Grubin. United States: PBS Paramount. Available online at pbs.org.

Aronson, Marc. *Robert F. Kennedy (Up Close)*. New York: Viking, 2007.

Kennedy, Maxwell Taylor. *Make Gentle the Life of This World: The Vision of Robert F. Kennedy*. New York: Harcourt, 1998.

Meachum, Ellen B. *Delta Epiphany: Robert F. Kennedy in Mississippi*. Jackson, MS: University of Mississippi Press, 2018.

Salinger, Pierre (editor). *"An Honorable Profession": A Tribute to Robert F. Kennedy*. New York: Doubleday, 1968.

Schlesinger, Arthur. *Robert Kennedy and His Times, 40th Anniversary Edition*. New York: Mariner Books, 2018.

Sorensen, Ted. *Counselor: A Life at the Edge of History*. New York: Harper, 2008.

Sullivan, Patricia. *Justice Rising: Robert Kennedy's America in Black and White*. Cambridge, MA: Belknap Press, 2021.

Thomas, Evan. *Robert Kennedy: His Life*. New York: Simon & Schuster, 2002.

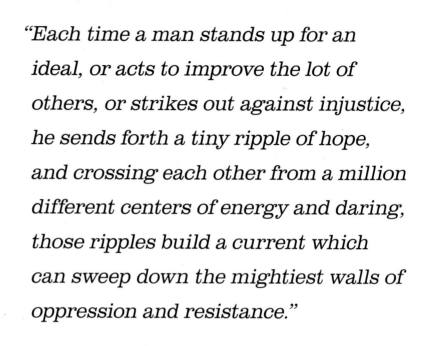

"Each time a man stands up for an ideal, or acts to improve the lot of others, or strikes out against injustice, he sends forth a tiny ripple of hope, and crossing each other from a million different centers of energy and daring, those ripples build a current which can sweep down the mightiest walls of oppression and resistance."

— Robert F. Kennedy

Day of Affirmation Address, given at the University of Cape Town, Cape Town, South Africa, 1966